Paris Underground

TAMARA HOVEY

ORCHARD BOOKS   NEW YORK

ACKNOWLEDGMENTS

I am indebted to the personnel of the libraries of Paris for their help to me during the preparation of this book. For their assistance in photographic research, I wish to thank Philippe Baur, director of the Photothèque of the RATP, and his colleagues Patrick Médard and Claude Carrau; Bernard de Montgolfier, curator-in-chief of the Carnavalet Museum, and Philippe Velay, curator of archaeology; Jean Dérens, head of the Bibliothèque Historique de la Ville de Paris, and his colleagues Luc Passion, Elizabeth Guilbaud, and Marie de Thésy; Jean-Claude Lemagny, curator-in-chief of the Department of Prints at the Bibliothèque Nationale; Sylvie Robin, archaeologist; Hélène Dusseauchoy of the Archives Photographiques de la Direction du Patrimoine; in the Public Relations Department of the RATP, Patrick Armand Vaintrub and Gérard Luche. For their general help, my thanks to Gail Saviola, Jean Trabant, and to my editor, Norma Jean Sawicki. I owe a special debt of gratitude to Michel Fleury, secretary general of the Commission du Vieux Paris, and to Jean Robert, director of research at the Centre National de la Recherche Scientifique.

PHOTO CREDITS

Arch. Phot. Paris/SPADEM: 8 (Seeberger, upper), 19 (Félix Nadar), 24 (Seeberger), 30 (Seeberger), 33 (Félix Nadar), 40 (Seeberger, upper and lower). Bibliothèque Historique de la Ville de Paris: 14, 20, 23 (lower), 25, 26, 38, 42, 47 (upper and lower), 50, 51, 56, 65 (upper and lower), 66. Bibliothèque Nationale: 2 (Philippe Benoist), 7 (Honoré Daumier), 8 (lower), 9, 12 (Honoré Daumier), 15, 16, 37 (le Génie Civil), 43, 54 (Honoré Daumier), 55, 62. Commission du Vieux Paris: 52. Cliché: Musées de la Ville de Paris © SPADEM: 57 (upper and lower), 59, 60 (upper). L'Illustration/Sigma: 13, 64. Musée des Transports: 22, 31. Rapho: 71 (Niépce), 77 (Doisneau). RATP: 3, 5, 6, 21, 23 (upper), 28, 29, 36, 41, 45, 46 (upper and lower), 48, 68, 70, 72, 73, 75, 81, 83 (upper and lower), 84 (upper and lower), 85, 86. Roger Schall: 76. Ron Renn: 10, 11 (upper and lower), 39, 53, 58, 60 (lower), 61, 63, 78, 79, 82.

Orchard Books, A division of Franklin Watts, Inc., 387 Park Avenue South, New York, NY 10016

Manufactured in the United States of America.
Printed / Bound by Horowitz/Rae. Book design by Mina Greenstein.
The text of this book is set in 12 pt. Garamond No. 3.
The illustrations are black-and-white photographs and prints reproduced in halftone.
2   4   6   8   10   9   7   5   3   1
Library of Congress Cataloging-in-Publication Data
Hovey, Tamara.
Paris underground / Tamara Hovey.   p.   cm.
Includes bibliographical references and index. Summary: Photographs, prints, and text depict the construction of the Paris subway.
ISBN 0-531-05931-6.   ISBN 0-531-08531-7 (lib. bdg.)
1. Subways—France—Paris—Juvenile literature. [1. Subways—France—Paris.]   I. Title.   TF847.P2H68   1991   625.4'2'094436—dc20   90-7980

To KATHRYN *and* LAURA

Contents

Introduction

ONE morning, in the early part of the century, in the city of Paris, France, a restaurant owner went down to his cellar to fetch some bottles of wine. But he came back empty-handed and no doubt cursing under his breath the men who were building the new subway—the Metro, as it was called for short, for it had taken the name of London's subway, the Metropolitan. In their zeal to fill in air pockets between a tunnel they had just completed and the earth around it, they had injected their cement further than they realized. It had dried, and the man found all his wine imprisoned in a huge solid block.

It was the sort of mishap that was bound to occur in the building of any underground transport system in Paris. The earth below the city was not the firm clay known across the Channel in England. It was a baffling honeycomb of abandoned stone quarries, of age-old river deposits that lay in wait to block digging machinery, of a seeping blanket of water that turned dirt hopelessly to slush.

The task of tunneling below Paris and under the River Seine, which divides it, was a colossal undertaking when it was begun almost a hundred years ago, in 1898. It was a half-blind foray into an unknown, underground world. It was performed in the face of floods, of fire, and at the cost of human life.

It was as well, though, an adventure into new techniques and into the world of France's past, whose dramatic traces could often be discovered by the mere turn of a shovel.

This is the story of that adventure.

Paris in the nineteenth century

1 · Before the Metro

IN early nineteenth-century Paris, there were no television antennas on the rooftops and no airplanes in the skies. As faraway as the Man in the Moon was the thought there would ever be a man on the moon. People cooked their meals over coal fires, they read and ate at night by the light of candles or of oil lamps, and the most up-to-date means of getting around town was a horse-drawn bus called an omnibus. During a brief period, almost two hundred years earlier, a public transport system of horse-drawn carriages had existed in Paris, but only for the privileged classes. The *omnibus*, a word eventually shortened to *bus*, was what the word implies, a "bus for everybody."

In 1828, when it appeared rumbling along behind swift horses, the omnibus was welcomed by Parisians, whose life was changing from what it had been in the relatively slow and quiet days of the previous century. Back then, Paris was small enough for people to walk. They could even get along in their own neighborhoods without ever stepping out of them. As in Paris today, only a half dozen city streets often separated one neighborhood from another, and each neighborhood was like a little village with its own butcher, baker, and candlestick maker. Artisans, who worked by hand with simple tools, labored in workshops at home.

By the time the omnibus appeared, Paris had grown in size and was no longer simple to cross on foot. Then, too, the year 1830 saw a new king—Louis-Philippe—placed upon the throne with the support of liberal bankers who championed him because he was a rich businessman like

Horse-drawn omnibuses on the Boulevard de la Madeleine

themselves. The old aristocracy of dukes and counts and princes had lost strength, a new aristocracy of money had taken over, and Louis-Philippe, who was called the Bourgeois King, personified it. As a general rule, he did not wear his crown or carry his royal scepter or remain in his palace. Walking the streets as any ordinary citizen would do, he wore a business suit and carried an umbrella. Under him, a new sort of France was taking shape—industrial France, France of the machine age. It was the birth of this machine age, some thirty years earlier, that was changing Parisian life.

Some artisans were forced to close their shops and work for wages. Machines could turn out goods more cheaply than the artisans could make them by hand, and their trade had begun to fall away. One could no longer stay in one's neighborhood night and day. More and more, work lay outside it—in factories or on new building sites.

Work lay in central offices of growing industries, too, where help was required from accountants, secretaries, managers, assistants, clerks, all of whom belonged to the lower middle class. Gradually, such salaried Parisians were forced to travel across Paris daily in one direction or another and travel in the most efficient way possible. There were always more needy people than jobs to be found; one had to get to one's own on time or risk losing it.

The omnibus was a boon to such Parisians. Only the wealthy could own a horse-drawn carriage or hire regularly carriages that stood at cabstands on various corners. An omnibus fare amounted to only a few cents, and it was within the means of the salaried worker.

Working people were not the only ones to take advantage of cheap public transportation. Fashionably dressed women, wearing broad-brimmed hats decorated with artificial fruit, would hail an omnibus on their way to the center of town to shop. Gathering their long, swaying skirts, they would mount the step to take a seat inside next to a law student, perhaps, or a horse breeder. A nobleman, fallen on hard times and no longer able to pay the wages of a private chauffeur, would find on the crowded bench beside him a bank employee or a music hall singer or a police spy trying to pick up tips by listening in on conversations.

Run at first by a single company, omnibuses became so popular that, in the space of two years, ten companies were operating in the city. During the nineteenth century, job seekers from the countryside moved to Paris. Nearby boroughs became part of the city, and the population of Paris grew from half a million to well over two and a half million. The omnibus companies grew with the city until, by 1900, they were handling the enormous job of feeding and stabling seventeen thousand horses in the capital.

During the same period, though, the streets of Paris did not grow to a comparable extent. By the time the century had reached its three-quarter mark, the presence in narrow quarters of so many lumbering omnibuses, dragged by often tired or skittish animals, created hopeless traffic tangles. They were not the only vehicles on the street. Sometimes omnibuses scraped the sides of buildings in order to make their way past private carriages or horse-drawn cabs or wagons loaded with produce. Since there were no traffic

The 5:00 A.M. *streetcar*

A crowded intersection at Boulevard de Strasbourg and Boulevard Saint Denis

rules and no stop signals, whichever was the biggest went first. The appearance, in the 1870s, of the streetcar—at first drawn by horses and later mechanically—only added to the confusion on the boulevards.

The disadvantages of the horse-drawn omnibus were slowly beginning to outweigh its advantages. It was costly to maintain a vast number of horses, and special horses were required. They had to be robust to keep their footing on the often slippery and uneven surface of Paris streets, which were made up of stone or wooden blocks or of hard-packed earth. And, since passengers were picked up at random, the animals had to be strong enough to withstand frequent starts and stops. In the competitive spirit of the times, the transport companies vied with each other for customers; they wanted their omnibuses to look nicer than anyone else's, and the horses had to be wine colored or trout colored so as not to show the dirt. In 1866, and still a practice today, the sale of horsemeat was legalized; nevertheless, horses were disposed of at a loss, and new horses had to be purchased every spring. Bad harvests drove the price of feed up, and, for the companies that ran them, horse-drawn vehicles became less and less profitable.

Above all, the public had begun to suffer. A person could sometimes wait over an hour for an omnibus, blocked in traffic elsewhere, only to see it at last rumble by, bearing a sign reading FULL. Accidents became more frequent, especially to pedestrians who tried to pick their way through the thick, disorganized traffic. In fact, one spot—the rue Montmartre where it intersected a boulevard at a diagonal—came to be known as the street of the "crushed" because so many people had been run over on it.

While Parisians cursed the problems caused by the very horse-drawn public transportation they had once looked upon as a blessing, members of the national government were lost in an argument with the city council of Paris. Beginning in the 1870s and during the following years, various proposals for a citywide subway had been discussed, and both sides had agreed that such a subway was vital. But they differed strongly on one question: Which of them should undertake the project? If it was deemed of general interest, they insisted, then the national government was the

"Gadzooks—full up!"

7

*The Chamber of Deputies, seat of the
National Assembly*

logical choice. The railroad owners, who hoped to see only a simple line that would get passengers as fast as possible in and out of the city to the great train networks they were building so profitably throughout France, lobbied for this choice. If, on the other hand, it was primarily of local interest, then the Paris city councillors should be responsible for the creation of a subway with sufficient lines and transfer points to serve the needs of the people who had elected them.

While these political interests and monied interests warred on—playing roles they would play, if with different faces, throughout much of the life of the Metro—the public was forgotten. Disgusted by the growing inefficiency and discomfort of overcrowded omnibuses and overflowing streetcars, some Parisians turned to an alternate means of transport—the riverboat.

Almost the same year the omnibus appeared on Paris streets, small water coaches had begun to paddle-wheel along the Seine to carry members of the royal court downstream to the palace in Saint Cloud. The first big riverboat lines made their appearance in the 1860s with the *Bateaux Mouches*—named after a neighborhood called La Mouche in the city of Lyons where the boats were built. These sturdy craft, equipped with steam engines and screw propellers, served convenient points along both banks of the Seine. They made it possible for people to move relatively close to their destinations in the city without the bother of surface traffic, and for the

A Bateau Mouche, a riverboat on the Seine

modest sum of twenty-five centimes for adults, no matter how long the voyage, while children under three traveled for nothing.

Soon the riverboat became a popular means of transport, especially on weekends in fine weather. At the peak of their popularity, toward the end of the century, riverboats collected some twenty-one million fares in one year. Passengers would sit in comfortable salons or on the open deck, their

A holiday crowd on the deck of a riverboat

The Cathedral of Notre Dame

eyes scanning the monuments of Paris—the Cathedral of Notre Dame, standing on its island in the river, or the Conciergerie where Queen Marie-Antoinette had been imprisoned during the French Revolution.

Nevertheless, Parisians discovered that water transport had its own drawbacks. Service was suspended during bad weather. On foggy days, the danger of collisions kept boats at the dock. And when the Seine froze, people who wanted to cross it were obliged to walk the river, pausing to warm up by buying hot chestnuts from vendors who set up their charcoal

The Conciergerie

braziers on the ice. More often, the river was swollen by rains and rose to heights that made navigation under the bridges impossible.

When they wanted to measure the extent of the Seine's rise, Parisians consulted the statue of the Zouave soldier on the Alma Bridge as one would consult a weather bureau. If the Seine had only covered the Zouave's feet, the river was passable. If the water had risen to the hem of his cape, boat service was suspended.

But, although over twenty years had gone by since the first discussions

*The Zouave soldier
at the Alma Bridge*

of a citywide subway had started, the opposing factions in the government were still arguing over who should build it. And frustrated Parisians, on the days when the boats shut down, had little choice.

The century was drawing to a close. Everyone knew by now about the proposed subway. Many wanted it, too; yet disgruntled Parisians had begun to complain that the project would never see the light of day. For so long, they had read articles about it in the newspapers. Drawings in magazines had depicted for them what route the new Metropolitan might take and how it might look. They had time and again been told that the only answer to often hopelessly blocked, disorganized city traffic was to take public transport off the streets. Yet, despite their desperate need for a subway, they saw not the slightest sign of the first subway car—except in the toy departments of the stores, where one could buy a tiny Metro train to put under the tree at Christmas!

In 1893, a journalist wrote: "As soon as the telephone was invented, children had theirs; a wire connecting two hollow drums covered with parchment. Now they have their Metropolitan and we still do not have ours."

The argument between city and state, nevertheless, was to continue for another two and a half years. And it might have gone on still longer but for an event that was to take place at the turn of the century and that would focus the eyes of the entire world on Paris.

"Full again. . . . I do believe they do it on purpose."

2 · First Steps on the First Leg

THE Paris World Fair was scheduled to open in the spring of 1900, and invitations had been sent to foreign governments. Before long, nations from all over the globe—from Siam to the British Isles, from Peru to China—would come to build pavilions on a vast fairgrounds covering two hundred fifty acres in the center of Paris. France would complete the Alexander III Bridge for the fair and two exhibition buildings that would later become permanent, the Grand Palais and the Petit Palais. Norway would construct an immense wooden chalet and beer tavern, while—on the banks of the Seine—the United States would erect an imitation of the Capitol building bearing a statue of George Washington on horseback and a dome surmounted by the American eagle.

The most recent inventions and the latest production techniques of each country would be displayed in the pavilions. Competition would be lively, and prizes would be awarded that could later lead to increased sales at home and abroad. The Baldwin Piano Company, for instance, whose piano had created little stir back home in Cincinnati, where it was manufactured, would receive such a prize, and soon concert pianists throughout the United States would be using the Baldwin piano.

But a world fair affected not only a nation's pocketbook; an international showcase for its industrial progress, it affected a nation's pride as well. Yet in the vital area of public transportation, what sort of progress had France to boast of? London had opened its subway as long ago as 1863. Budapest, the capital of Hungary, had recently built one. In New York City, trains

The Paris World Fair of 1900

13

rode on bridges in a rapid transit system called the "elevated." It was suddenly clear that Paris must have the first leg, the first line, of a subway completed in time for the Paris World Fair of 1900. The national government gave way, and on November 22, 1895, the minister of public works granted the City of Paris the right to construct the subway.

In order to create a new subway system, many different groups had to work together under an overall plan, and such a plan was developed over the next few years by a commission set up for the purpose. A private company known as the CMP—the Paris Metropolitan Railway—was to be granted the right to run the future subway. The company would be responsible for the organizing and financing of the secondary work, such as the construction of the cars and of station entrances, and later it would pay the city a percentage of the fares it took in. The city would be responsible for the primary work—the tunnels and platforms—and handle the financing out of loans.

To head the primary phase, the *Ponts et Chaussées*—the department of bridges and roads—provided the city with a chief engineer who was to be responsible for the designing of the network and for the construction of its tunnels. His name was Fulgence Bienvenüe. He was in his forties when he accepted the position, and he did not know then that the Metro would occupy him—and passionately—until his retirement in his eighties.

Bienvenüe had long since proven his worth to the city. Early in his career, he had lost an arm in an accident on the tracks during the building of a railroad. He ignored his handicap and rose steadily in his profession. By the 1890s, he had several impressive works to his credit. He had reshaped the course of the Avre, the Loing, and the Lunain rivers to bring their waters to Paris. He had cut through the city to create the broad Avenue de la République. And he had installed a cable car that ran up and down a hill in a neighborhood in the north of Paris known as Belleville.

A thirteenth child of Breton parents, Fulgence Bienvenüe had received a taste for the classics from his father, a notary public who translated Latin authors in his spare time. The discipline that could be acquired by studying

Fulgence Bienvenüe

The Belleville cable car

in ancient Greek the works of Homer and of Plato was his. At the same time, he was capable of brilliant flights of imagination—a trait, oddly enough, reflected in his first name, Fulgence, which is taken from the Latin *fulgere*, meaning "to flash brightly."

Physics class at the Ecole Polytechnique

In his serious and single-minded attitude toward work, Bienvenüe carried on a tradition of the great French engineers of the nineteenth century—of Alphand, who had created the parks and gardens of Paris; of Belgrand, who had constructed its sewers. He belonged, as they had, to an intellectual elite formed by a Paris school noted for its rigorous training, the Ecole Polytechnique.

Bienvenüe was so absorbed in his work that he was indifferent to personal comfort. He rose daily to a cold bedroom because he never took the time to install heat. Though electricity was available, he used kerosene lamps. The men who had worked under him in the past had admired their chief for the swift, simple solutions he brought to knotty problems, and soon new teams would name him Father Metro.

In designing the Metro's early lines, Bienvenüe followed, as closely as possible, the path of the main streets. His principal reason for doing so was the relative simplicity of digging tunnels just below ground level.

Another reason, however, was the existence of a law by which a property owner owned his land to the center of the earth. This meant that, if the city wished to dig under buildings, it had to pay the owners for rights-of-way. Throughout the history of the Metro, land was sometimes rented or bought, and often buildings themselves were bought. But one way to limit expenditures was by digging under the streets, which were owned by the city itself.

The Metro's network, in its first stages, was to consist of six lines, which included a line that would run north-south, another east-west, and another that would circle Paris. The most important, at the moment, was the east-west leg, which was to be completed in time for the world fair, along with two small offshoots, one of which would lead directly to the fair. When the city received Bienvenüe's plans, building companies submitted competing bids for the work. The city then chose separate companies to handle the construction of tunnels simultaneously on different segments of the line. The building companies in turn hired the work crews, and there was always available to them a pool of unemployed.

Some would be experienced diggers who had worked on construction jobs in Paris or in coal mines up north. The majority would be unskilled French laborers, sometimes joined by immigrants who had found their way from colonies in Africa to seek a better living in Paris. Or here and there among them might be former journeymen—traveling artisans who moved from town to town. They had once enjoyed the freedom and the peace they discovered in unspoiled nature and the absence of anyone but themselves telling them what to do. But, just as the city artisans had, they had seen their trade dwindling.

All of these men were glad to find jobs on the Metro despite the flying dust on the work site in the summer and the dank cold of the tunnels in the winter. In most work, when the job was done, one had to search for another, but the building of a subway could go on for years and years and bring in a steady income.

In November 1898, two thousand men, divided into shifts that worked around the clock, began constructing tunnels on different segments of line 1. The line was to run from an eastern gate of Paris, the Porte de Vincennes, to a western gate, the Porte Maillot. It would cover a distance of about six and a half miles, and the authorities insisted that it be in operation in the short space of less than two years. The diggers would have to tunnel out the dirt ahead of them at the difficult rate of thirty-five thousand cubic feet every twenty-four hours to meet the deadline. In addition, when they found them in their path, they would have to reroute sewers or electric cables that lay beneath city streets.

The use of dynamite, which would have made the work proceed more easily and more swiftly, had been ruled out in many areas by the city authorities. They believed that shattering explosions would be bad for public morale. Although they had realized early on how much they needed a subway, Parisians had also read articles in the past promoting elevated lines for the Metro and describing underground tunnels in lurid terms. At the sight of the dark, deepening breaches in their streets, they began to grumble uneasily at the prospect of soon being invited to descend into "the depths of hell."

As the tunnel work proceeded, the men followed a pattern. First they dug a pit in the earth with their picks and shovels. Then they lowered wooden ladders into it so that they could come and go while, on its dirt floor, they laid out tracks for their equipment. They installed electricity to run the hoists that would carry away the dirt and to power the lights that would help them see what they were doing as the underground work progressed.

When this preliminary work was completed, the men dug— horizontally—into one side of the pit, to create a tunnel. And they used, in the beginning, the "shield" method. This method had been tried for the first time in 1825 during the building of a tunnel near London under the River Thames by Marc Isambard Brunel, a French-born engineer later knighted by the British Crown. It is still used in building tunnels today.

The shield was made of metal and was the size and shape of a subway

*Working under the
shield at the Place de
la Concorde in* 1899

tunnel. Jacks driven by water pressure enabled it to move forward. The shield's main purpose was to hold up a section of dirt tunnel until that section was lined with a metal ring. This ring, assembled at the rear of the shield, was about a yard long.

Diggers worked at the front of the shield under a beak that "shielded" them from falling dirt and rocks. When they had cut out a length of tunnel about a yard long with picks and shovels, they jacked the shield forward. As it inched ahead, it left behind a hollowed-out stretch of dirt tunnel. Into this space the men gradually fitted the metal ring, in this way reinforcing that section of tunnel so that it could no longer cave in. Then the men repeated the process, digging out a new section, jacking the shield forward, and fitting another metal ring into place. A succession of these rings, which were joined tightly and finished with masonry, became the final wall of the Metro tunnel.

The enormous quantity of dirt and rubble created by the Metro works was hauled off to the countryside by rail and by river barge.

Carting away the dirt by river barge

Geological layers found later in building the Crimée station

Soon enough, however, Bienvenüe discovered that the shield method could not always be used. Unlike the firm, smooth clay that lay under London, the earth below Paris was made up of deposits built up over the ages by movements of the sea and of the River Seine. On one level was white chalk, on another sand, on another green and blue dirt, and the whole was interspersed with great banks of stone and topped by still more dirt, in which fragments of oyster shells gleamed.

These layers, which they saw for the first time, were a delight to geologists, whose work is the study of the structure of the earth. The variations in texture of the deposits, however, made the earth uneven and hindered the shield's progress. Sometimes the shield stopped functioning altogether, and precious time was lost. The discovery of such layers, of course, was but one of the surprises, among others on future lines, that Paris earth would hold for Bienvenüe. At the moment, his "quickly flashing" mind sought, for those areas where the shield was inefficient, alternate methods of tunnel construction.

Instead of metal rings, which required the shield, strong wooden galleries were built to hold the dirt tunnel in place. Later, the galleries were

Lining a tunnel with wood

Building a tunnel just below street level

finished with concrete and cement and sealed with mortar to keep the wood from rotting. Or a tunnel just beneath the surface of a street was dug and the street resurfaced. Soon this "cut-and-cover" method, as it was called in the United States, would be used widely in the building of the New York subway, as it had been used earlier on the London Metropolitan.

While problems underground were being grappled with, others arose aboveground. One day, an accident occurred on a work site near the Arch of Triumph. A tunnel was under construction, and fifty-five yards of its ceiling caved in. As the ceiling fell, the street above was deprived of its support and fell, too. It dragged with it trees and gas lampposts, and two passersby were injured.

The event increased the already mounting irritation of Parisian merchants with the Metro works. They had not even seen yet the huge carcass of a station tunnel that would one day soon temporarily occupy the entire breadth of the Boulevard Saint Michel in the Latin Quarter, where students lived. But they had seen enough, and they brought suits against the city

The Arch of Triumph

for disrupting the streets in front of their shops so that they had lost their customers.

City authorities pressed even harder for completion of the line so that urban life could return to normal. Bienvenüe calmly delivered to the authorities periodic progress reports, marked occasionally by a certain dry

Tunneling under Paris

humor that was sometimes lost on them, then hastened underground to rejoin his men.

He felt at home working with those men underground. In fact, he referred to himself as a "simple workingman." Moreover, the dark regions in which they all struggled, hidden from the world above, were teaching him much. "The essence of underground constructions," he later wrote, "is their utter ingratitude toward their authors. It is quite right to say that, if difficulties have been truly and fully overcome, the final result must no longer bear a trace of this, and the men who conquered those difficulties have no other choice than to be taken at their word."

By April 1900, Bienvenüe was able to announce to the authorities that he had met his deadline. It was an impressive feat; he had completed the tunnel work on the first line in a record seventeen months. The French still remember this striking, brilliant achievement. Now the workers aboveground hastened to catch up with him.

Subway cars, manufactured in the north of France, had not been delivered to the newly created workshops at Charonne near the Porte de Vincennes. Rails had not been laid or signals installed, and work on stations was unfinished. Feverish activity took over this phase of the work, but even by the end of June it was not completed. Yet test runs were successful, and the Metropolitan company decided that a sufficient number of stations had been completed along it to put line 1 into operation. Cutting across Paris from east to west, the stops were Porte de Vincennes, Nation, Gare de Lyon, Bastille, Hôtel de Ville, Palais Royal, Champs Elysées, Porte Maillot.

On July 19, 1900, the first line of the new subway opened for business. It was a blistering day. At the offices of the newspaper *le Figaro* on the Champs Elysées, the thermometer registered over a hundred degrees in the shade. Parisians, seeking to escape the heat in the coolness of the tunnels, forgot their fears and went to neighboring stations to buy their first Metro ticket, then board the new trains and ride in comfort to the world fair in full swing at the Champ de Mars.

But the opening of the Paris Metro that day was—as an event—ignored. In the first place, the Metropolitan company, fearing that too many people

An underground ticket booth

Arriving at the fair on a moving sidewalk

might try to crush into the Metro, decided to avoid all publicity. No elaborate statements were released to the press, which hardly mentioned the subway that day, and no inaugural ceremonies were held.

More important, it was the very event that had spurred the government at last to build a subway that overshadowed that subway's birth. The Paris World Fair of 1900 was a great spectacle. Electricity was a comparatively recent invention, and it had been used lavishly to create an illuminated fairyland on the banks of the Seine.

Even before the Metro opened, an electric train, whose line had been extended expressly for the fair, brought visitors to the edge of the grounds. The novel device of moving sidewalks carried them toward an entrance. Inside, over the weeks, glittering groups could be spied, where King Leopold of Belgium might be present. Or the Shah of Persia. Or all the mayors of France, attending a formal banquet at which three thousand waiters and kitchen help served four hundred cold salmon, thirty-five hundred hens, twenty-five hundred pheasants. . . . Indeed, throughout the six months the fair lasted, it offered so much to dazzle the eye that Parisians forgot the Metro that brought them to it.

But this was strangely unimportant. While not everyone realized it at the time, that July 19, 1900, was a significant day. Although the riverboat and the horse-drawn omnibus were at the height of their operations, that day marked the beginning of their downfall. The older, less efficient modes of public transportation would gradually give way before the marvel of the subway.

To be sure, there was no real subway at the moment. Only eight stations had opened on the first line, while future lines had not yet left the stage of the drawing board. Moreover, Fulgence Bienvenüe and his men were only dimly aware of the challenges that lay ahead, hidden in the unpredictable world of Paris underground. Yet even through the tunnels they had already completed, there had ridden, in the first two weeks alone, over a half a million passengers. The Metro was on its way.

A symbolic funeral for the last omnibus in 1913

The Arènes de Lutèce

3 · Digging into Problems

As Bienvenüe and his engineers dug further underground, new problems arose. On line 1, they had worked in earth that was close to the surface. Now they were moving under hills, under a canal, into underground territory for which sometimes even the city possessed no maps. The one thing people could tell them was something they already knew: For nineteen centuries, the earth below Paris had been carved up by builders, and the earliest of those builders had been Romans.

Before Paris existed, the land now called France was inhabited by barbarian tribes known as Celts. In 58 B.C., a Roman general, Julius Caesar, set forth to conquer the Celts, whom he dubbed Gauls. During the Gallic Wars, a settlement of wooden huts called Lutetia, which had grown up on the island where Notre Dame now stands, fell to the Romans. It was inhabited by a tribe called the Parisii, who later gave their name to Paris. After the war, the victorious Romans stayed on in Lutetia, which the Parisii themselves had destroyed to prevent its capture, and created a new city in their own grand style. They built stone roads, aqueducts, public buildings and baths, and an arena on the Left Bank—known today as the Arènes de Lutèce—for theatrical and gladiatorial spectacles.

For this extensive construction, the Romans needed building materials and found them beneath the ground. There was limestone that could be cut into strong, solid blocks, and there was a substance called gypsum that could be used to make the purest form of plaster, plaster of Paris. Five hundred years later, the Gauls saw an end to Roman rule with the invasion

A stone quarry in northeast Paris

of barbarian tribes that included the Franks, who would give their name to France. They, too, drew upon the rich deposits below, digging ever deeper into the rocky underground pits—the quarries—to extend the city above, century after century.

In the beginning, the quarries had lain outside the city limits, but, as Paris extended its boundaries, they came to lie beneath it. The quarries were worked in some areas as late as the 1860s. Forty percent of Paris underground is honeycombed by their abandoned stone galleries. Twisting and turning in a complex maze, quarries run for some one hundred eighty miles under the city. They go down so deep in certain places that, if a modern ten-story building were placed in a quarry pit, only the roof would show.

Over the years, criminals eluded the police and smugglers evaded customs officials by slipping through the quarries. On the eve of uprisings, revolutionary groups held secret meetings in their shadowy galleries. During the eighteenth century, graves in overcrowded cemeteries were dug up. The bones were transported at night in hearses covered with a pall, followed by priests chanting the service of the dead. They were deposited where they lie today, in limestone quarries reached by an underground passageway beneath the Place Denfert-Rochereau. Eventually, the bones were arranged by type in tightly packed layers along the dim corridors of these underground burial chambers, the Catacombs.

When Bienvenüe was extending line 7 of the Metro through the Chaumont Hills in the north of Paris, he found quarries in his path. In a park in the hills, stone grottoes rose near a waterfall. They were part of old plaster quarries that lay underground. When workers abandoned a quarry, they filled the galleries with rubble, and later buildings, parks, and streets were built on the fill. It was impossible for the Metro's engineers to know what lay under the ground, and they approached the city's quarry department. They wanted to learn the depth and extent of the quarries beneath those hills. Gigantic stone pillars that held up a quarry's "sky"—its ceiling—were often left intact by quarry workers when they abandoned a

The Catacombs

pit. And, to aid in the construction of their tunnel, the engineers wanted to learn the location of such pillars.

Le Service de l'Inspection des Carrières—the quarry department—had been set up in the eighteenth century when heavy rains softened the earth and caused a road or a hill or even an entire building at times to cave into the quarries below. Since its formation, the department has carried on the colossal work of consolidating the quarries under the capital and of mapping them out, one by one. Nevertheless, in the 1910s, the department had no maps for the Chaumont Hills or any information about abandoned quarry pillars.

The engineers—including Louis Biette, who would work under Bienvenüe for a quarter of a century—searched elsewhere. Finally, they met a former surveyor who had marked out the area at one time. The notes and figures he gave them described primarily only the upper region of the quarry but enabled them to start the digging.

As they cleared away the rubble, they came upon plaster quarries where immense pillars of gypsum rose up from such a depth that, in a photograph of the era, a man standing on the quarry floor is no more than a small figure. They would be forced to build their tunnel—as if on stilts—on concrete piles. Quarry dirt, made up of loose stone and clay, packs down, as does snow, under pressure, and it would be difficult to construct in such dirt.

Over the months, the men worked to build their tunnel, which led, on and off through quarries, from the Chaumont Hills to the Place du Danube. They dug deep, circular holes that they filled with concrete to form their piles. They spaced the piles close together to give maximum support to the tunnel. Nevertheless, when the men, using the wooden gallery method, began to build the tunnel, it tilted. The engineers ordered the tunnel reinforced with a new support that went straight down to the floor of the quarry.

As the work progressed, quarry pillars in their path were cut through and rested on the tunnel. They exerted great pressure on its walls, as the surrounding earth did, too. Sometimes the pressure was so great that posts in tunnel frames were crushed into the ground. Overhead wood split. Vaults sagged. And even after the wooden galleries were sealed with concrete, pressure would cause chunks of concrete, sometimes more than a foot thick, to break off along the tunnel wall.

As each crisis arose, the engineers sought to resolve it. To support the tunnel to the utmost, they piled against it, in a Y-shaped system, which distributed the pressure, the largest amount of dirt possible. They anchored the tunnel to other stout quarry pillars, which it took diggers searching with pick and shovel painstaking weeks to find.

When the tunnel at last held firm in one part of the line, greater problems could arise in the next. At the Place du Danube, the men encountered the *carrières d'Amérique*, the "quarries of America," so named because, in times past, their gypsum had been exported to provide America with plaster of Paris. Three vast layers of gypsum had once been dug out of these quarries. A gigantic cavern of gaping galleries and loose quarry dirt had been left behind, and the Metro tunnel would somehow have to bridge it.

In areas where it was impossible to build underground tunnels, the Metro had been built on bridges. At various points throughout Paris and over the River Seine, aerial bridges exist. Bienvenüe's engineer, Louis Biette, had begun to construct such bridges, and one of them spans the Boulevard Pasteur, named after the celebrated French scientist who invented pasteurization.

But to build an aerial bridge underground was difficult, especially in a plaster quarry made up of soft gypsum. Nevertheless, that is what Bienvenüe and his engineers did. They bored down through the gypsum until they reached hard limestone rock. And they anchored their tunnel to the rock floor of quarries that soar to the height of a ten-story building. The result is that, beneath the Place du Rhin et Danube today, where rarely the tourist sets foot, there lies an extraordinary piece of engineering art— an underground elevated railway. Young apprentice engineers produced a

The Metro bridging the Boulevard Pasteur

model of it for study and exhibit at the time; it showed the two train tunnels of the Place du Danube station supported by giant piles.

Not only did quarries cause problems for the engineers as they dug deeper, so did underground water, and it existed in several forms. Once a small river called the Bièvre flowed over the Left Bank of Paris before it joined the River Seine. Over the years, it was used by dyers . . . by tanners . . . by glue and soap factories. It grew so polluted that, little by little, it was covered over. By Bienvenüe's day, it ran underground as part of the sewer system, as it does today. The existence of a second river, the Grange-

Batelière, for a time thought to have flowed past land where the Paris Opera House stands, was proven to be only a legend. Wet sands, however, found underground in this region, drew their moisture from a very real source—underground water traveling through a permeable layer of sand and rock, called the aquifer.

The two tunnels of the Place du Danube station on giant piles

During the building of the Metro, this blanket of underground water was perhaps the engineers' worst enemy. It seeps below Paris, through sievelike holes in the aquifer, to empty into the sea as the Seine does. It is fed, via the upper layers of the earth, by rains and melting snows. Water from the aquifer turned up often as the men dug deeper, causing problems whenever it was encountered. It created wet spongy dirt that was difficult to handle and in which there was always a danger of a tunnel's slipping.

Workmen often spent long hours trying to keep moisture from this water layer at bay. They put special covers over the joints of their wooden galleries. Or they stuffed hay, as tightly as possible, into the cracks between the posts and the waterlogged earth. In many areas where the aquifer exists, Bienvenüe was obliged to set up permanent drainage pumps, which still function day and night in modern Paris to keep earth around tunnels dry.

Finally, there were underground springs—a blessing today to those Parisians who are lucky enough to live in a neighborhood where they need only turn on faucets in their homes to enjoy pure, fresh springwater. They were hardly a blessing, however, to the engineers on the Metro works in 1901 when they were extending line 3 under the Saint Martin Canal to connect the République station with the Parmentier station.

The Saint Martin Canal lies in the northeastern part of Paris. Today, as in the past, it carries water from the River Ourcq to the capital, where

Damming the Saint Martin Canal in 1901

it is used for industrial purposes and for cleaning the streets. The canal is also used by pleasure boats that ply their way through its locks. In the early part of the century, however, the canal carried cargo boats, and Bienvenüe chose midsummer, when cargo traffic was light, to extend his line. The city drained the canal at the tunnel's projected underground crossing point and agreed to keep it dry for fifty days. Once again faced with a deadline, diggers worked around the clock.

One night, when they were digging eighty feet below ground level, the men struck limestone rock with their picks. A geyser of water shot up and flooded the floor of the pit. They turned on pumps that were capable of carrying off water at a rate of a hundred thousand gallons an hour, yet could not dry up the pit. The workers brought in emergency pumps and—days later—another pump. But the pumps had little effect because the flow was increasing now as the opening below grew ever wider under the force of the escaping water. Soon, carried on the water, small boulders came crashing into the pit, and the engineers sent for a diver.

The man dove below and discovered a powerful underground spring running between the layer of hard rock the men had pierced with their picks and a softer layer of rock below it. The softer layer, which was made up of boulders, pebbles, and sand, was being torn apart by the rushing water. Work on the tunnel could not continue until a way was found to block off the spring.

The engineers invented a huge "cork" made of quick-setting concrete reinforced with bits of iron and cast iron. Through a pipe that extended above the water level, they poured this concrete below. Divers guided it toward the opening in the rock from which the water was gushing; the concrete set, and the underground spring was cut off.

Bad weather sometimes hindered the progress of construction of the Metro. During the winter of 1910, it rained continually. The Seine rose to such heights that it rippled around the tip of the beard of the Zouave soldier on the Alma Bridge. Paris was flooded. All but one line of the Metro was flooded, as was the riverbank Bercy power plant, which supplied

The Saint Martin Canal today

The Seine under floodwater

The city under water during the flood in 1910

the Metro with electricity. The devastating event brought tunnel work in low-lying areas to a standstill.

Once during the flood, rainwater entered a tunnel on high ground and exited from a Metro station on a lower level. Immediately, cranks sent letters to the city blaming Bienvenüe for water in their streets. In general, however, tunnels drew large quantities of floodwater off from the streets. As Bienvenüe calmly answered the cranks, the Metro was serving the city as an excellent drain. When spring came, workers were forced to do extensive repairs on tunnels that had been damaged during the great flood.

As the floodwaters receded

Digging a tunnel in front of the Grand Hotel and the Paris Opera House

Bienvenüe and his engineers had to deal once again with underground water when line 3 reached the Place de l'Opéra. Here, on the square, stood the beautiful Paris Opera House, designed and built forty years earlier by the architect Charles Garnier. Across the street was the Grand Hotel. On the other side of the square, the broad Avenue de l'Opéra, lined with shops, swept down toward the Seine.

In this spot, the plans called for the crossing of three lines—the one currently under way and two future lines. To save labor, the three tunnels at the crossing point were to be built at the same time. Underground water from the aquifer, however, lay in the area, and the sandy earth was water-logged. Before Garnier could begin building the foundation for the opera house, he had kept pumps going day and night for more than seven months in order to drain the land. Bienvenüe avoided this expensive and lengthy procedure by enclosing his three Metro tunnels in an immense, watertight, concrete block.

The pit the men had to dig to hold this block was so large that Parisians soon named it "the hole." A journalist described it as "a great mouth which will stand wide open, ready—on gala nights at the Opera or during street parades or popular celebrations—to devour the crowds who have the misfortune to approach its jaws." After eleven months of labor, Bienvenüe completed one of his most ambitious and spectacular works in this hole: three tunnels on different levels—separated by metal flooring—crossing in the center of the square.

A rare problem arose with the extension of line 4 when plans called for digging a tunnel under the Quai Conti. On this quay stood the Institute, meeting place of the celebrated writers, artists, and scientists who belonged to the elite French Academies. When the members heard of the plans to build the Metro under them, they declared there would be no noisy rumblings beneath their conference rooms. So respected were the academies, and so influential, too, that Bienvenüe was forced to change the original plans. He had to lead the line in a less convenient direction, and to cross the river twice instead of once, so that the discussions of those whom the French call the Immortals would not be disturbed.

Crossing a river underground was risky in this early part of the century, when safety measures on any work site were in a backward state. Sometimes accidents occurred; in one, five diggers were drowned, and the other diggers went on strike.

The building company in charge had agreed to a special clause in its contract with the city: If the company finished the work ahead of schedule, it would receive a bonus, but if it went over schedule, it would be docked.

The Institute, meeting place of the French academicians

When the diggers struck, the company immediately brought in laborers from the countryside and installed them in huts on the riverbank. It hired police to guard the new men—the "yellows," as the striking diggers called them—so that the strikers could not prevent them from working. Throughout the building of the Metro, there was no repetition of an industrial accident of so serious a nature; nevertheless, the memory of it hung over diggers who worked on any underwater line.

The engineers had to deal not only with the same hazards the diggers did, but also with the amount of time the complicated work of tunneling under a river could take. When Brunel built his underwater tunnel in England, he began it in 1825 and finished it eighteen years later. Since Brunel's day, however, the need to mine ore under riverbeds had produced a new procedure: the use of compressed air. It would speed up the tunnel work considerably.

When compressed air was forced down a shaft into a working chamber that rested on the river bottom, it drove the river water out of the chamber. Then, even though the chamber itself was surrounded by the river, diggers could work inside the chamber as if they were on dry land.

When Bienvenüe and his men led line 4 across the Seine, they sank a great long metal tube under the riverbed; this was the tunnel through which the trains would travel. In the work, they used compressed air. But they also used a method for building an underwater tunnel that had never before been tried.

In the method, a prefabricated section of the future tunnel—called a caisson—was constructed on the riverbank, then launched into the river, where a tugboat hauled it out into position. The men poured concrete over the caisson, and the weight of the concrete sank the caisson to the river bottom. Then they forced air through a shaft into a working chamber attached to the base of the caisson, and it drove out all the water. Diggers then climbed down an iron ladder in the shaft into the chamber below.

The working chamber was like a coverless box turned upside down. Standing on the riverbed, the diggers attacked the bottom with picks,

Building a caisson on the banks of the Seine

ABOVE: *Launching the caisson*   BELOW: *Hauling the caisson into position*

sometimes using smokeless powder to blow up rock. Over months, removing the earth beneath the caisson little by little, they inched the caisson ever deeper into the bed of the Seine.

The men worked eleven-and-a-half-hour shifts in the cramped, sealed quarters. Their feet slipped in the sticky gray mud of the riverbed. The air was steamy and hot. When they used too strong an explosive charge to break up rock, knifelike splinters of rock sprayed the chamber. A telephone allowed them to communicate with fellow workers above the river. Otherwise, they were cut off from the rest of the living world.

At the end of the shift, the men hoisted their buckets of dirt and rock and climbed back up the shaft. The pay for "tube" work was eighty centimes an hour—almost double pay for a digger. The workers, however, had to eat and sleep in a special dormitory near the site, to be on call in the event of an emergency in the tunnel.

Entering the compressed-air shaft

The working chamber

A dormitory for underwater tunnel workers

When they had buried the caisson beneath the riverbed, the men abandoned the working chamber. They filled the chamber with concrete to anchor the caisson, emptied out water that had helped to steady it, and dismantled the compressed-air shafts. Then they began work on the next caisson. Five caissons, linked together, were used to build the underwater tunnel on line 4. It ran from the Place du Châtelet on the Right Bank to one of the islands in the Seine—the Ile de la Cité—and from the island to the Left Bank.

The line had almost reached the Left Bank, however, when a problem of dramatic proportions arose at the Place Saint Michel. Once again, the underground water of the aquifer was responsible. At this particular spot, the Orléans railroad ran under the quay, and the tunnel would have to be built under its tracks. It was impossible to sink caissons—the tracks were in the way. The men would have to dig out a tunnel with picks and shovels. But they could find no way of handling the slippery mud that underground water created all around them. Digging a tunnel through it was like trying to dig a tunnel through mayonnaise. Even the coolheaded Bienvenüe had to admit they had reached an impasse, although his quick imagination was already at work.

Soon he ordered the men to dam off the Seine in the area that lay between the last caisson and the riverbank. Then he had sixty long probes sunk into the mud vertically. Connected to each was a set of twin pipes. After reducing the temperature of a solution of calcium chloride to minus eleven degrees Fahrenheit, he had the chemical poured into these pipes. The solution traveled down one pipe and up another, and in the process gradually reduced the temperature of the surrounding earth. At the end of forty days, the mud was frozen solid, and the diggers could hack at it with their tools.

Calling upon creative thinking of this nature, Bienvenüe was able to see this crossing of the Seine completed in a little over four years. That thinking, too, combined with the body of his superior accomplishments throughout his work on the Metro, would earn him, later on in life, four

The freezing system at the Place Saint Michel

awards of the Legion of Honor. It would earn him, as well, another honor that had special meaning for him—the inauguration in 1933, on the newly named Place Bienvenüe, of the Bienvenüe Metro station.

Bienvenüe would accept all his honors with grace, but would also take care to state:

> "Where the artist stamps his work with his own personality, the engineer is often led to think of himself as producing a work that is impersonal. This is because, in the area of technique, the actual concrete idea may arise from his solitary pondering, yet the form it finally takes on is the result of the efforts of a great many people. This community of effort is shown to the highest degree in the Paris Metropolitan."

LIGNE N° 14
OUVERTE AU PUBLI
DE LA
Pte DE VANVES
A LA
PLACE BIENVENÜ
A MIDI

The inauguration of the
Bienvenüe Metro station

*Archaeologists at the Bastille
Metro works in* 1899

4 · Journey into the Past

THE work of Bienvenüe and his assistants contributed much over the decades to the science of civil engineering. Even during the early days, their work contributed to another science, as well. That science—archaeology—deals with the discovery of objects that have lain hidden in the earth for long years. Bones of the prehistoric animals, for instance, who once roamed riverbanks where cities now stand. Shattered pieces of a graceful vase fashioned more than two thousand years ago. Or, dropped long ago in a marketplace or in the street, ancient coins nibbled around the edges by wear and stamped with faces unfamiliar to us. To the layman, such objects might seem of little worth, but the archaeologist will study them and perhaps learn something that was never known before about the art and life of people who lived before our times.

Even in the days before construction on the Metro started, scientists suspected that Paris was rich in underground archaeological treasure. In 1897, the city decided to establish its Commission du Vieux Paris—a commission for the preservation of "old Paris"—to aid in the discovery and safeguarding of that treasure. The Metro works arrived on the scene a year later. As the workers tunneled into the earth in nearly all parts of the city, they created mammoth digging sites archaeologists were able to make use of almost from the start.

During the extension of line 1 of the Metro, as it moved in a northwesterly direction from the Gare de Lyon, a worker struck his shovel against

The base of the Tower of Liberty in the Square Henri Galli today

what appeared to be no more than a pile of dusty stones. Archaeologists from the commission, however, soon arrived on the site in their black suits and tall black hats. They recognized in the stones the base of an old fortified tower called the Tower of Liberty. Up until then, there had been only minor finds during the construction of line 1. Here, however, was a rare discovery. The diggers had tunneled into the heart of French history—the spot where once had stood the grim prison, the Bastille.

For centuries, the shadow of civil injustice had hung over the Bastille. By means of a mere letter—the sinister *lettre de cachet*—and without any formal charge, a person could be thrown behind bars for an indefinite period. Unless a prisoner could afford to pay for decent food (as very few, such as the celebrated writer Voltaire, could do), he was left to waste away in his chains.

"Royal Prison: Entrance—Exit"

Storming the Bastille

A Gallo-Roman sculpture found during the building of the Cité station in 1906

While France lay under the domination of the nobles and the clergy, the prison endured. But in the eighteenth century, the common people made their voices heard. Inspired by the ideals of the American War of Independence, they called for "no taxation without representation," along with other fundamental human rights. In order to crush the despotic regime under which they suffered, however, they felt obliged to destroy the symbol of its power, the Bastille. Under the banner of *Liberté-Egalité-Fraternité*—Freedom, Equality, and Brotherhood—on July 14, 1789, they stormed the prison. They seized its ammunition supplies and freed its inmates and, with this gesture, started the French Revolution. In the coming year, when the people had succeeded in overthrowing King Louis XVI and establishing a republic, they tore the prison down stone by stone. Then they danced in the square to celebrate Bastille Day, as Parisians have been celebrating it in their streets every July 14 since.

The base of the Tower of Liberty—one of the Bastille's eight original towers—was carefully removed from the Metro site. Eventually, it was placed where it stands now, on the Right Bank in the gardens of the Square Henri Galli. And this important find was followed by others as the Metro tunneled on through Paris underground.

Discovered mingling in the dirt with relics from ancient times and garbage from the previous century were the remains of buildings from the Middle Ages. Along the rue de Rivoli today, for instance, one can spy the erect, tall bell tower of an eleventh-century church, but no church. Yet, uncovered during the digging on line 1 were stone underpinnings of Saint-Jacques-la-Boucherie, the church that had once borne into the sky this old belfry.

For centuries, Paris had protected itself against foreign invaders by ringing the city with fortified stone walls. And during the building of Metro lines on the Right Bank, diggers came upon important traces of an old city wall that had been constructed under Charles V in the sixteenth century.

Around 1910, cutting Paris down the middle with new north-south lines, the subway drove great furrows through the capital, unearthing among many discoveries one perhaps only an archaeologist would have considered important—cinders. A study of these cinders revealed that they had been produced from limestone building blocks under high heat. Their location—the island called the Ile de la Cité—strengthened the view that the Gallo-Roman city of Lutetia (now the heart of Paris) had suffered a fire during the early centuries of Roman rule. This find was extraordinary because it was tangible proof of an event that had taken place in the far distant past. That fire, however, was not the first to have swept over this island.

During the Gallic Wars, the Parisii, who dwelled on the island, fought a bloody battle with the Romans. The Parisii were fishermen and expert sailors. They built fine boats that enabled them to dominate the waterways of the region. But their long, blunt, poorly tempered sabers were no match for the short, pointed swords of the Romans. Though the Parisii fought with courage, they were eventually put to rout. And the victorious Romans rode off, leaving behind them the smoking ruins of Lutetia.

The two enemies who figured in the battle that day lived together afterward, of course, to build a new civilization on the smoking ruins— the Gallo-Roman civilization. And clues to this civilization were discovered in rare abundance during work on the north-south lines. There were blocks from public buildings, funeral slabs, monumental sculpture. There were bas-reliefs of ancient figures who seemed to grow out of the stone from which they were carved. One such bas-relief, of three Gallo-Roman fishermen, was found in 1906 in digging to build the Cité Metro station tunnel and was photographed at the time on the site.

A multitude of smaller objects from the same era was discovered as well, from coins to bits of pottery to safety pins with which Gallo-Romans fastened their flowing robes. And there were inscriptions. Sometimes these Gallo-Roman inscriptions, written in stone in Latin, were legible. Sometimes, though, working out the meaning of one was like decoding an enemy message in wartime, the enemy in this case being Time, which had worn

ABOVE: *A Gallo-Roman sculpture*
BELOW: *A decoration on a Gallo-Roman column*

A Gallo-Roman façade at the Monge Metro station

away letters. Often, too, a sentence would break off in the middle, when the stone itself broke off. But even when it was only partially successful, such decoding was important. It could occasionally bring to light heretofore unknown historical fact.

Not only inscriptions served this end. Long ago, the River Seine had occupied a larger bed than it does today, but the city had expanded, narrowing it. The Metro works uncovered three earlier quays, each one lying deeper in the earth and set further back. From these discoveries, scholars were able to trace the history of the Seine.

In the same way, archaeologists continued to draw their own conclusions as the Metro works carried on. When coins unearthed in the digging grew lighter, it was a sign hard times had come to the Gallo-Romans, for less precious metals were being used. A rapid change in design in pottery and glass was an indication of the speed with which Roman art had come to dominate that of the early Gauls. When an area on the Left Bank not far from today's Latin Quarter turned up nothing, although discoveries had been plentiful in nearby areas, even that "nothing" had meaning: It hinted at the existence of an agricultural belt that had supplied early Gallo-Romans their food.

But, if the Metro works helped shed light on historical fact at times, at times their finds produced only mystery. Discovered in a ditch near the site of the Bastille, and measuring a little under seven inches, was a terracotta burial statuette of King Osiris, the Egyptian god of the dead. But how had this royal stranger arrived in such an unlikely spot? Had the artifact been fashioned long ago in a Paris atelier? Had it been imported from the Middle East? Had it belonged, perhaps, to a prisoner who had let it fall accidentally from the stone ramparts of the Bastille? No one was able to answer such questions at the time, and no one can answer them still.

Cannonballs were sometimes discovered by the Metro workers on the site of the Bastille, which had defended itself with a great cannon known as the *Grande Mademoiselle*. They were not a common occurrence in other

A statuette of King Osiris found near the site of the Bastille

An old French cannonball similar to those fired during the Hundred Years' War

regions, but during the work on line 7 at the Palais Royal, a cannonball one day rolled to the feet of diggers tunneling near a spot where once had stood the old city gate of Saint Honoré. It was immediately presumed to be a fifteenth-century cannonball and a souvenir of a famous battle in which a great French military leader had been wounded.

During the Hundred Years' War, England, taking advantage of the civil strife that divided the kingdom across the Channel, invaded France. After a military triumph at Crécy, the English established dominion over northern France. The French fought back over the years and, during a battle one of their armies was waging near the old Saint Honoré gate, they were met with a rain of arrows and a volley of cannonfire. Wounded in the thigh, that September 1429, was their strong-willed and daring commander, a teenager called Joan.

Joan of Arc was a shepherdess from Domremy who claimed to have heard heavenly voices urging her to drive out the invaders and unify France. She understood the mood of the French, routed by foreigners and wounded in their national pride. She helped restore that pride by her acts and by

Old stones from the Bastille on display in the Bastille station

her powerful faith, but it cost Joan of Arc her life. She was convicted of heresy by the Church and burned at the stake at the age of nineteen.

In the twentieth century, archaeologists felt a similar pride in the relics of France's past they were accumulating. They wanted to see them adorned with suitable labels and enshrined, for the benefit of future Metro passengers, at the locations on which they had been discovered. The construction companies, however, by and large opposed the idea. The establishment of such shrines might necessitate detours in the tracks and delay the tunnel work, which would cost them money. And in the end, a rare old cannonball . . . three Gallo-Roman fishermen . . . an Egyptian deity were carted off to the museum for good.

All the same, standing on the platform of the Bobigny/Place d'Italie line at the Bastille station today, one can see on exhibit stones from a wall that once lay on the east moat of the Bastille fortress. And, from another platform in the same station, one can take the Metro on line 1 westward. As the train gathers speed to head on toward Saint Paul, it nears a tablet on the tunnel wall to the left of the train. Gleaming fleetingly in artificial light before it disappears from sight, the tablet pinpoints the old location of the Bastille's Tower of Liberty—a historic spot that might have remained hidden forever were it not for the Metro's chance archaeological diggings.

Those diggings continued, diminishing only with the crisis in construction after World War I. Well before that, however, a catastrophe occurred on the Metro that put in question its very existence.

*The statue of Joan of Arc
at the Place des Pyramides*

*The Couronnes
platform on
August 10, 1903*

5 · The Couronnes Disaster

THE night of August 10, 1903, was creeping toward dawn. For hours, a tall column of thick black smoke had been billowing out from a stairway that led beneath the street. Soon now, out would come the firemen—shaken, blackened, too—and finally the bodies. On August 12, the front page of the *Petit Journal* carried the headline:

LA CATASTROPHE DU METROPOLITAIN

Eighty-four men, women, and children had died in a fire underground. The majority of them had died in the Couronnes station on the Porte Dauphine/Nation line, and the rest in the tunnel or in the next station up the line. The grim news filtered out slowly because smoke had formed for the firemen a poisonous, impassable wall throughout the night. In a few days, Fulgence Bienvenüe, who had gone to the scene to investigate, would furnish the city authorities with details of the events that had led up to the catastrophe.

At the Barbès station at 7:05 P.M., he reported, a short circuit caused a fire to develop in one of the forward motors of an eight-car train. After discharging the passengers, the train continued, powered by its rear motors. It reached the Combat station, where a second train came to its aid after also discharging its passengers. Coupled, the two empty trains traveled toward the end of the line. They passed the Couronnes station and had almost reached the next station, Ménilmontant, when the fire flared up and spread rapidly throughout the cars. The motormen escaped, but smoke traveled back through the tunnel and reached the Couronnes station, where

Entrance to the Couronnes station today

After the disaster

a full train had been ordered to stop. The passengers were evacuated and were urged to leave the station, but they lingered, demanding a refund on their tickets. Suddenly, the lighting system failed, and the station was plunged into darkness. Panic set in, and those who did not reach the exit were overcome by smoke and died of carbon monoxide poisoning.

It was a tragedy of overwhelming proportions, and a mood of mourning seized the nation. Telegrams of condolence poured in from all over the world. A solemn mass was performed at the Cathedral of Notre Dame, and services for the victims were held on the square before the nearby barracks of the Municipal Guard. The stricken crowd listened to the words of Premier Emile Combes:

"This sad page follows, in the history of humanity, other pages equally sad. In the eyes of a pessimist, it could pass for a condemnation of science. For it is science, in its never-ceasing, forward struggle as it searches for the unknown, which is responsible. At stake in this struggle are men's lives; the outcome is progress. It would be as vain as it would be damaging to humanity to thwart its march."

Services for the victims on the square before the garrison of the municipal guard

City officials listening to Combes's speech

The words were a plea, in a sense, not to abandon work on the Metro, whose first eight stations had opened just three years before. But the newspapers were already writing of the *"métro-necro"*—the death train—and asking when the city itself would collapse into the tunnels. During the two weeks following the tragedy, the average number of passengers on the Metro fell by half. In England, where the subway had been built at a greater depth and where trains were isolated in one-way tubelike channels, terrified Londoners deserted the tube for buses.

After Couronnes, one question was uppermost in everyone's mind: Had the disaster been unavoidable? If so, there was clearly no future for underground transportation. The fate of the Metro, however, would lie for many in the findings of a board of inquiry that the city immediately set up to investigate safety in trains and in stations and to uncover, if possible, the party responsible for the accident. Bienvenüe's work was not in question as much as the Metro's ability to function safely after the tunnels were

On the right, Bercy electricity factory on the Seine

completed. And, since a short circuit had been the apparent cause of the disaster, among the first people questioned were representatives of the electric power companies.

The representatives argued that they were not present to defend the use of electricity in the Metro, even though it had been attacked on every side since the disaster. The government itself, they noted, had approved the employment of electrical power on the subway and had formalized that approval by law in March 1898. In addition, as more passengers were packed into the cars and as more cars were added to trains, the extra burden on motors had led to their overheating and had increased the incidence of minor fires; clearly, the overloading of trains was not the responsibility of the power companies. Finally, on the night of the disaster, if the motorman had broken electrical contact between the motor and the power rail, the flames would not have spread.

The *wattman*, as the motorman was called in French at the time, was immediately summoned—"this piece of dirt," a journalist, quoting from a La Fontaine fable about a scapegoat, wrote wryly, when an indignant public placed all blame on the motorman. The board of inquiry learned to its surprise that short circuits were a common occurrence on the Metro. The *wattman* cited a figure of forty to fifty incidents each month without serious consequences. Thus, he told the board, there had been no special cause for alarm on the night of August 10. Moreover, an attempt to isolate the power rail had failed because water used to put out the fire had acted, of course, as a conductor. As the discussions continued, it became clear that electrical equipment throughout Metro trains was poorly insulated.

The work of the board of inquiry was beginning to seem like the overturning of a stone that reveals all manner of unsightliness beneath. "The stench alone is sufficient to make people sick," declared the press, and lack of proper ventilation in the stations was also brought out into the open. Questioned, too, was the absence of an alarm system, as well as the absence of a backup system for the station lights, whose electric boxes had caught fire from the burning train.

Inspecting wooden cars in use at the time of the fire

The twisted and blackened remains of trains 43 and 52 were a stark reminder that the construction of the cars themselves was a key issue. Finally, companies responsible for the manufacturing of the cars were called in for questioning. It was common knowledge that Metro cars were made of materials that burn easily—fir or varnished pitch pine—while their electrical elements were insulated with rubber or gutta-percha, both inflammable. But following a disastrous fire on the Overhead Railway in Liverpool, England, two years earlier, both the Central London Railway and the Hochbahn in Berlin had produced new models that were better insulated and therefore safer. Why, the board demanded, had the French companies not followed suit? The men replied that, in the first place, it took a long time to produce a new model. "As for the model currently in use," they added, "it was costly to manufacture, and the capital invested in it cannot be sacrificed."

Once again, the conflict between monied interests and the public interest was making itself felt. The *Assiette au Beurre*, in its article of August 22, stated:

> The authorities have had in effect the guilty lack of foresight to abandon the Metro to the capitalists whose motto is: Minimum of cost and security, maximum profit. And it is always "progress" which is asked to pay for the broken china, although it is no guiltier than the Metro motorman or the film projectionist at the Bazar de la Charité or the stagehand at the Opéra-Comique.

At the latter two locations, serious fires had also occurred.

In the end, the board of inquiry did not single out any one guilty party. Before filing the matter away, it concluded: "The catastrophe of August 10th was due to one of those incidents which normally ought not to take place in any electrical enterprise but which are inevitable given the present state of our technology."

The findings of the board proved to be of immense value, for they caused new and stricter safety measures to be ordered by the prefect of police. Alarm systems were to be installed. Stations serving several lines were to be equipped with more and larger doors. Special lights indicating exits were to be set up in all stations, while emergency lighting was to be placed in both stations and tunnels. Fire hydrants were to be provided in every station and inspectors assigned for every group of five stations to direct operations in case of an emergency.

As for the car manufacturers, they would soon produce an improved model. Gradually taking over from the Thompson Double, with two motor cars, front and rear, would be trains carrying several motor cars and built on an electrical system that would be in worldwide use by the 1930s. This "multiple unit" system of automatic control had been invented by Frank Sprague, an American engineer. Trains called the Sprague, the Sprague-Thompson, or the Little Sprague would ride on the Paris Metro for three-quarters of a century.

Sprague's system took the strain off any one motor, and the low voltage it employed eliminated the danger of overheating. To further reduce strain on motors, engineers installed "bogies," which allowed trains to take curves smoothly, as if on a swivel. In the future, all-metal driving cabs would come into use, followed by all-metal trains.

With these radical improvements in safety, it was hoped that the public, sorely shaken by the Couronnes disaster, would gradually regain its confidence in underground transportation. It did, and the Metro carried on. It moved from what Bienvenüe described as the "precarious period" of its birth to the "superactive period" of its growth. And, in the coming years, it developed into a highly complex network that was still so simple and logical that any Parisian could easily find his way around it.

Constructing the Metro around 1904

The modern Metro is so simple
and logical that any Parisian
can easily find his way
around it.

Passengers arriving at the Saint Michel station on the first subway in the world to use rubber tires

6 · Riding toward the Future

As the Metro expanded in the early part of this century, it gradually became intertwined with the lives of Parisians. Its stations were moments in their biographies—the stop where they used to get off for school, the stop where they had always transferred to go to a grandparent's apartment, the stop where they had exited over the years to meet a best friend. And, as the French made the Metro their own, it was written about in books, sung about in songs, and depicted on film.

In the early part of the century, Metro entrances, decorated by the art nouveau work of Hector Guimard, sprouted throughout the city. Their cast-iron plant stems soared skyward toward a drooping flower that embraced a light globe. They represented a rebellion against classical form and an expression of "art for the people." They soon became the distinguishing mark of the Paris Metro. Guimard's entrances can still be found in certain neighborhoods of Paris, and one is on exhibit in the Museum of Modern Art in New York City.

During World War I, which began in 1914 when the Germans invaded France, some Metro stations were damaged by bombs—Saint Paul, Corvisart, Campo Formio, and Couronnes. The enemy had entered the country via the coal-mining regions of the north and deprived the French of the fuel they needed to produce electricity. Because they relied on coal imports, the French cut down on their power use, and the Metro departed from platforms lit by only a dozen dim, yellowish bulbs. In the face of bombardments, aerial Metros—easy targets for enemy aircraft—were run on

A Metro entrance designed by Hector Guimard

low blue interior lights that lent the trains an eerie look as they traveled over the river, almost invisibly.

Streetcar employees went to the front and left streetcars for the most part unmanned, while city buses were taken away by the army. The Metro was almost the sole public transportation available in the capital. Benches were ripped out of subway cars to make room for more passengers. Women replaced men as train attendants, and, to reduce the number of attendants needed, an automatic system of opening and closing doors was introduced on the Metro.

At the start of the war, Bienvenüe, a reserve officer in the engineering corps, had asked to serve, but the city considered him more useful at his post. However, although line 7 was extended to the Palais Royal during the war years and some little progress made on other lines, tunnel construction in general suffered from lack of personnel and material.

In the decade that followed World War I, rising costs slowed construction in all areas. But along with this slowdown, there appeared a growing crisis in housing that would affect the Metro's development. During the first three decades of the century, many working people, unable to find affordable housing in the capital, moved into the suburbs while still retaining their jobs in the city. And, although the population of Paris remained relatively stable, the suburban population increased from under one million to over two. The growing number of suburban workers who needed to travel daily to and from Paris spurred the government to extend the Metro's lines beyond the city limits.

The inaugurations of new extensions connecting the capital to its suburbs were important events during the 1930s. They marked the growth of a once closed-in, fortified city into a thriving and populous region called *le Grand Paris*—Greater Paris. During his brief retirement before he died in 1936, Fulgence Bienvenüe made regular appearances at such inaugurations. Indeed, they would have been strangely incomplete without the presence of the man early diggers had called Father Metro and who had become recognized by now by everyone as the Father of the Metro.

A Metro station converted into a factory by the Nazis

In 1940, during World War II, the Nazi Germans invaded France and occupied Paris. They took over line 11 of the subway and transformed the Place des Fêtes station into a factory for the production of airplane parts. At the Porte des Lilas station, they ripped out tracks, cemented over the roadbed, and installed their machinery on the platform.

A sign in a Metro telephone booth during the Nazi occupation of Paris reads "Use Forbidden to Jews."

During the Occupation, the Nazis enforced their racial laws in the Metro. Jews were not allowed to ride in any but the last car, which came to be known as the "synagogue." And, along with the use of public facilities aboveground, the use of telephone booths in the Metro was forbidden to Jews. As they had sheltered them during World War I, the Metro's deeper stations served Parisians as a refuge during air-raid alerts in 1944 when the Allies were bombing the capital to liberate France.

During World War II, the underground tunnels of the Metro served as a stage for another sort of "underground"—the French Resistance. In

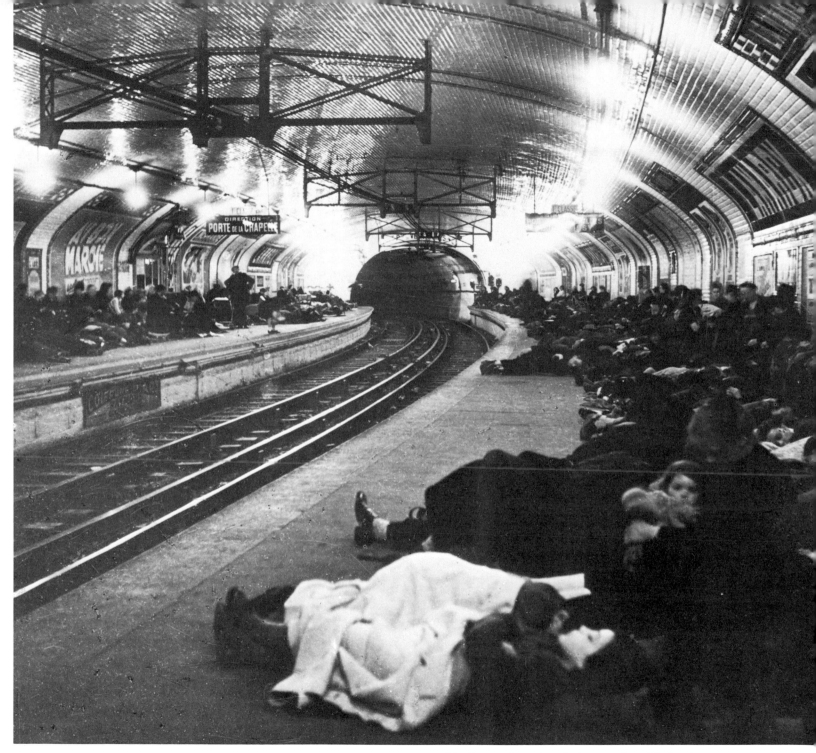

The Lamarck station during an air-raid alert in 1944

1941, Pierre Georges, using the name Colonel Fabien, belonged to this secret, illegal movement. He was twenty-one when he killed a Nazi on the Barbès-Rochechouart platform with two pistol shots, then escaped up the Metro stairway to lose himself in the crowds. His act was a key factor in causing the French Resistance to move into the offensive against the Nazis.

In the Catacombs below the Place Denfert-Rochereau, the Resistance established headquarters for operations: sabotage, sniping, and street fighting. They established another post directly under the Prefecture of Police. A tunnel there, leading to the Cité Metro station and initially used for the transfer of troops, had been overlooked by the Nazis. Soon, Resistance fighters were contacting their comrades in other parts of Paris via the tunnels, and there developed in the Metro a human network mirroring its own.

When the Nazis blocked the exits of the Prefecture of Police in 1944, the police who had gone over to the Resistance escaped by disappearing into the underground tunnel below. After World War II and the defeat of

*The Combat station was renamed
in honor of a famous Resistance fighter.*

The station named for the
United States' thirty-second president

Nazi Germany, the Combat station was renamed for Colonel Fabien, while another station honored an American wartime president, Franklin Delano Roosevelt.

Construction on the Metro fell into a decline for almost fifteen years after the war. Lines that had been started before the war were completed, but no new work was begun. It was a difficult economic period, and the Metro, which the government had taken over from the private company, suffered from lack of funds. Other sectors demanding government support were granted priority—war-damaged cities, railroads, ports.

Another reason for the decline was the automobile. A hundred years earlier, although he could not afford the price of it, many a Parisian dreamed of owning a carriage of his own. Now he longed to own a car and was able to buy one on credit. Soon there appeared on Paris streets small Citroëns and Renaults and Peugeots, each with its often solitary, proud driver. Middle-class Parisians turned their backs on underground transportation, and it seemed as if the Metro's popular days were over.

Little by little, however, Parisians realized that they could never do without their Metro; the automobile itself brought the message home. Drivers sat for hours behind the wheel inching, bumper-to-bumper, across their city and remembered the Metro on which they might have made the same journey in a swift twenty to thirty minutes. Just how vital the Metro was to their lives was made dramatically clear to Parisians whenever the Metro workers went on strike. Then city streets became a solid mass of seemingly motionless vehicles, and the sidewalks swarmed with weary pedestrians.

In 1959, a reawakening to the Metro's importance to the capital inspired a period of new activity and one that has lasted up to the present day. The Metro had already brightened and renovated its stations. Now, granted fresh funds, it was able to modernize its cars. The 1960s saw realized on three Metro Lines a revolutionary notion for increasing the efficiency of subway trains—rubber tires. A new train, the "Metro boa"—with cafeteria, video area, and no doors dividing the cars—is now in the test stage.

Over the years, new building techniques were developed. Ordinary cement gave way to water-resistant brands, and the shield gave way to a "jumbo shield" fitted with a compressed-air system and weighing hundreds of tons. During the 1960s, the Metro network itself developed. Begun in 1962 and completed in 1981, a series of regional express lines built in collaboration with the railways and known as the RER enables Parisians to travel in record time to the suburbs. In 1988, a new station—Cluny-La Sorbonne—was opened in the Latin Quarter for university students.

Despite the enlargement of the Metro's network, however, the work of

Fulgence Bienvenüe of almost a century ago is vividly present in the modern Metro system. "It is curious to note," writes Jean Robert in his *Notre Métro* (*Our Metro*), "that the metropolitan network which we know today is almost exactly the network planned in 1907. Much more, the first draft of it in 1901 already contained the seeds of most of the operations which have been seen to fruition on the urban network since."

The work of the early engineers is present in the tunnels themselves. In 1928, Bienvenüe looked back on thirty years of struggle with the special problems building tunnels under Paris posed. And he wrote that the practical solutions he and his men had discovered had made unnecessary any major alterations later on. "This is as it should be," he added, "for you cannot start a metropolitan over again."

From the early days when Bienvenüe and his men built the first tunnel through which the first motorman drove his train with simple hand valves alone, the Metro has traveled a great distance, and Parisians have followed it. Now, cars they ride in at peak hours are brought out of garages by

A control center

remote electronic guidance from control centers—at Vincennes, Denfert-Rochereau, Bastille. A control center can cut off electric current almost the instant an accident on the tracks is signaled to it by a train conductor on his high-frequency telephone.

While Paris once lagged behind other countries in public transportation, the Metro now has fifteen lines, more than any other subway system in the world. Over a billion Parisians a year ride the Metro.

Recently—in ways natural and familiar to Parisians—the Metro has become a world unto itself,

with underground shops at the Opéra station,

underground photographic exhibits at Saint Augustin,

Rodin's *Thinker* at Varennes,

underground music at Auber.

Even the personnel of the Paris transport authority—the RATP—who seek to improve their technical knowledge of the Metro at the *Centre de perfectionnement technique du Métropolitain* near the Parc Monceau, go through

an abandoned Metro entrance,

walk down an abandoned tunnel, and listen to lectures underground.

But if the earth below Paris is no longer the unexplored territory it once was, and if today workers are no longer obliged, as once they were, to ward off moisture in wooden galleries by stuffing the cracks with hay, does it mean the Metro's underground adventure is over?

Or is some present-day Fulgence Bienvenüe, with a flashing imagination of his own, standing on a station platform tonight in the Latin Quarter? And is he turning over in his mind the thought that the Metro he is waiting for will connect up soon to an express train that will speed him through a tunnel under the English Channel to bring him to London in a breathless two and a half hours? Who can say?

One thing is certain. The story of the Metro—like the story of progress itself—has as yet no end.

CLUNY
LA SORBONNE

A new Metro station in the Latin Quarter

Bibliography

Research for this book was done in Paris from French sources that have not been translated into English. I have listed the major sources.

Biette, Louis. *Les chemins de fer urbains parisiens.* Paris: J. B Baillière et Fils, 1928.

Gérards, Emile. *Paris souterrain.* Paris: Garnier, 1909.

Guerrand, Roger-Henri. *L'aventure du métropolitain.* Paris: Editions La Découverte, 1986.

Hervieu, Jules. *Le Chemin de fer métropolitain municipal de Paris.* Paris: C. Béranger, 1908.

Hurtret, André. *Le Métropolitain et les vestiges souterrains du vieux Paris.* Paris: A. Poidevin, 1950.

Lacordaire, Simon. *Histoire secrète du Paris souterrain.* Paris: Hachette, 1982.

Robert, Jean. *Histoire des transports dans les villes de France.* Paris: Musée des Transports urbains, 1974.

————. *Notre Métro.* Paris: Musée des Transports urbains, 1983.

Roland, Gérard. *Stations de Métro.* Paris: RATP/Christine Bonneton, 1986.

Verpraet, Georges. *Paris, capitale souterraine.* Paris: Plon, 1964.

Virgitti, Jean. *Les installations du chemin de fer métropolitain de Paris.* Paris: L. Eyrolles, 1933.

COLLECTIONS

A la mémoire de Fulgence Bienvenüe réalisateur du métropolitain. Paris: Perceval, 1937.

Lutèce, de César à Clovis. Paris: Société des Amis du Musée Carnavalet, 1984.

le Métropolitain. Paris: Hôtel de Lamoignon, 1988.

FOR FURTHER READING

Cudahy, Brian J. *Under the Sidewalks of New York.* Lexington, Mass.: The Stephen Greene Press, 1988.

Green, Oliver. *The London Underground.* London: Ian Allan, 1988.

Maurois, André. *A History of France.* London: Jonathan Cape, 1953.

Index